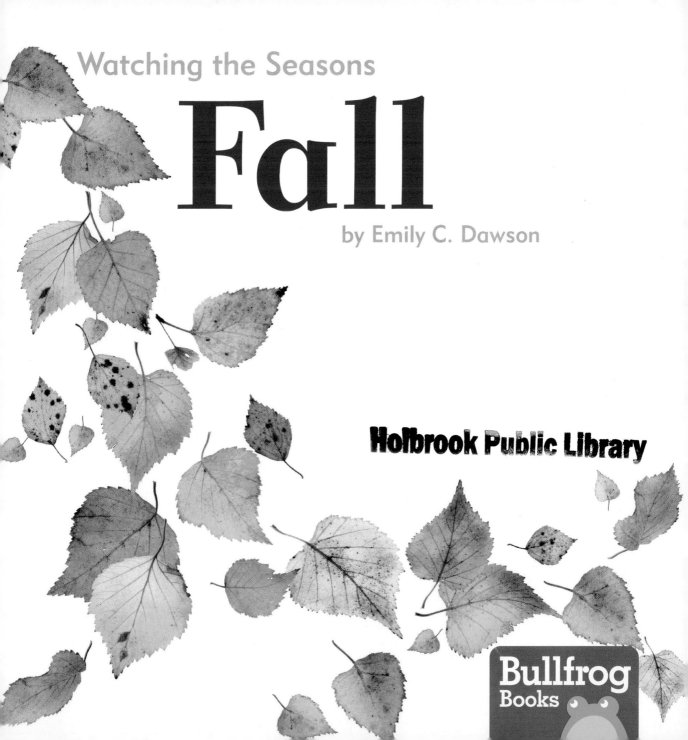

Watching the Seasons

Fall

by Emily C. Dawson

Bullfrog Books

Ideas for Parents and Teachers

Bullfrog Books let children practice nonfiction reading at the earliest reading levels. Repetition, familiar words, and photo labels support early readers. Here are some tips for reading with children.

Before Reading
- Discuss the cover photo. What does it tell them?

- Look at the picture glossary together. Read and discuss the words.

Read the Book
- "Walk" through the book and look at the photos. Let the child ask questions. Point out the photo labels.

- Read the book to the child, or have him or her read independently.

After Reading
- Prompt the child to think more. Ask: What is fall like where you live? What do you like to do in fall?

Bullfrog Books are published by Jump!
5357 Penn Avenue South, Minneapolis, MN 55419
www.jumplibrary.com

Library of Congress Cataloging-in-Publication Data
Dawson, Emily C.
 Fall / by Emily C. Dawson.
 p. cm. — (Watching the seasons) (Bullfrog books)
Summary: "This photo-illustrated book for early readers describes how fall weather affects the actions of animals, the growth of plants, and the activities of people. Includes photo glossary"
—Provided by publisher.
Includes bibliographical references and index.
Audience: Grades K-3.
ISBN 978-1-62031-016-8 (hbk.)
1. Autumn—Juvenile literature. I. Title.
QB637.7.D29 2013
508.2—dc23
                                        2012009118

Series Editor: Rebecca Glaser
Series Designer: Ellen Huber
Photo Researcher: Heather Dreisbach

Photo Credits
All photos by Shutterstock except: Dreamstime, 3t, 6, 8, 16, 19, 23bl, 23tr; SuperStock, 5, 14, 18, 21, 23tl

Printed in the United States of America at Corporate Graphics in North Mankato, Minnesota.
7-2012 / 1124
10 9 8 7 6 5 4 3 2 1

Table of Contents

Fall is Busy

In fall, nature is busy.

Get ready!
Winter is coming.

In fall, squirrels search.

They find acorns.

They hide them for winter.

In fall, geese
fly south.

They fly in a V.

They go to a
warm place.

Mexico

In fall, monarchs migrate.
They fly to Mexico.
It is warm there.

In fall, leaves drop.

Winter is too cold for leaves.

12

In fall, people rake.
Ben plays in the
leaf pile.

He covers Sam.

In fall, farmers harvest.

The corn is tall.

It is ready to pick.

In fall, kids carve pumpkins.

Tia makes a scary face. Boo!

In fall, kids dress up.

Elly is a bee for Halloween.

What do you do in fall?

Watching the Seasons

Spring

Summer

Winter

Fall

Picture Glossary

Halloween
The evening of October 31, when kids go trick-or-treating.

migrate
To move to a different place, usually to get away from cold and find more food.

harvest
To bring in crops that are ripe.

pumpkin
A round, orange fruit that grows on a vine.

23

Index

To Learn More

Learning more is as easy as 1, 2, 3.

1) Go to www.factsurfer.com

2) Enter "fall" into the search box.

3) Click the "Surf" button to see a list of websites.

With factsurfer.com, finding more information is just a click away.